To Ripon
~ with love

A glimpse into the past

Memories of childhood holidays in Ripon

Margaret Lancaster

FOR BOB & WENDY
A light hearted
reminiscence.

Published by

WOOD END PUBLICATIONS

2009

Wood End
Publications

Copyright © Margaret Lancaster, 2009

ISBN : 978-0-9563134-1-6

Contact : **woodendpublications@googlemail.com**

Printed by : **thinkink**
11-13 Philip Road
Ipswich
Suffolk
IP2 8BH

ACKNOWLEDGEMENTS

I should like to acknowledge the family help and support which I have received; from my son-in-law Peter Hills for hours of 'computer work', also to my daughter Greta Hills and granddaughter Rebecca Hills for proof reading.

Thanks to John Lancaster, my son-in-law, for background information and to my daughter Susan Lancaster for general support and encouragement.

I am indebted to Christine Roberts for background information regarding Australia, to Jacqueline Mason and also to Janice Brigham and Gillian Douglas of Lindisfarne.

CONTENTS

INTRODUCTION

I was brought up between the Wars on a farm at Bradley near Skipton, North Yorkshire, where life was lived at a slower pace and mechanical aids were few. Because my father was self-employed we children rarely went away on holiday as there were cows to milk and feed, sheep to fother, and hens to see to. A day at Morecambe or Blackpool now and then was about the limit of our travel experience. Therefore, when I was asked to accompany my cousin Gladys to stay with her relations in Ripon it seemed like a dream come true. The memories of those unexpected holidays are still fresh in my mind, and are recorded here, backed up by a few facts concerning the places we visited.

For about four years in the late 1920s we must have gone to Ripon each year in August , though I have forgotten the exact dates. In this account I have recorded also a little of my early life, since this too now seems to belong to a past age — but it was the world we knew. Our visits to Ripon were the highlights of our childhood and were looked forward to eagerly throughout the year.

The wheel has now turned full circle. By a quirk of fate it happens that my daughter and son-in-law have lived and worked in the vicinity of Ripon now for many years. Inevitably, when I visit them and pass the familiar scenes of my youth, I find the memories of those former days crowding in on me.

The people who provided this opportunity are long gone, but those wonderful holidays in Ripon remain as fresh in my memory as if they were yesterday. I dedicate this book to their memory as I recall those never-to-be-forgotten happy days spent once a year in Ripon in Lickley Street.

Margaret Lancaster
(née Throup)

The Journey

The journey from Bradley to Ripon in the old Trojan car.

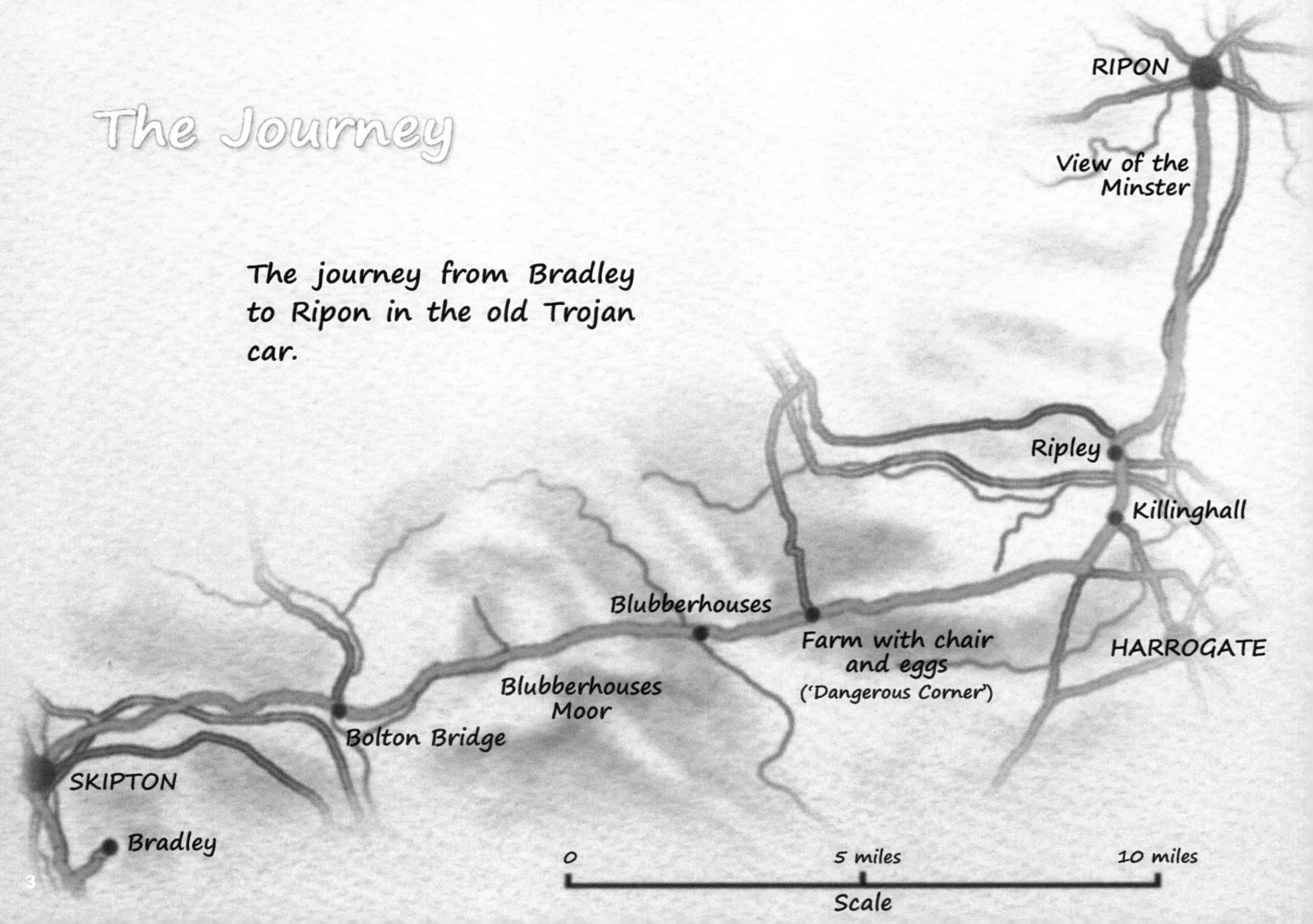

RIPON

View of the Minster

Ripley

Killinghall

HARROGATE

Blubberhouses

Farm with chair and eggs ('Dangerous Corner')

Blubberhouses Moor

Bolton Bridge

SKIPTON

Bradley

0   5 miles   10 miles

Scale

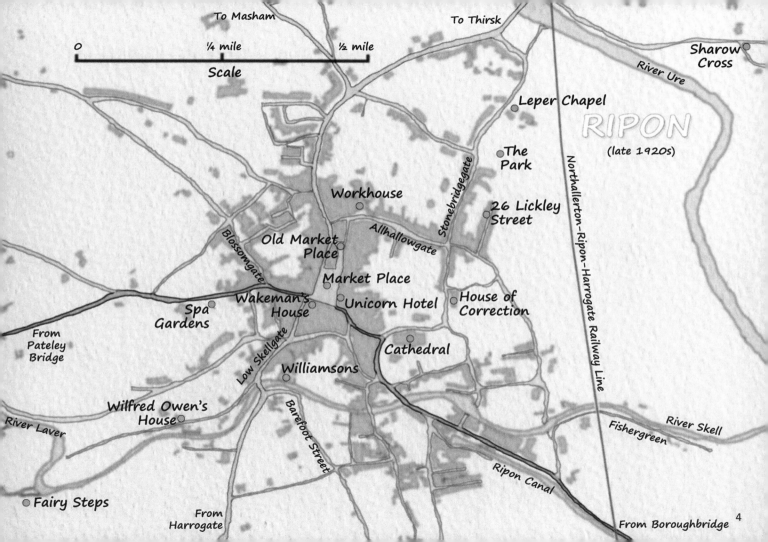

To Masham

To Thirsk

Sharow Cross

0   ¼ mile   ½ mile

Scale

River Ure

Leper Chapel

RIPON

(late 1920s)

The Park

Workhouse

Stonebridgegate

26 Lickley Street

Blossomgate

Old Market Place

Allhallowgate

Northallerton–Ripon–Harrogate Railway Line

Market Place

Spa Gardens

Wakeman's House

Unicorn Hotel

House of Correction

From Pateley Bridge

Low Skellgate

Cathedral

Williamsons

Wilfred Owen's House

Barefoot Street

River Laver

Fishergreen

River Skell

Ripon Canal

Fairy Steps

From Harrogate

From Boroughbridge

4

HIGH BRADLEY

Moor cottage is the building on the right.

MEL

We lived in Corn Mill Lane, Bradley, but when I was about six years old my father received a letter offering him the tenancy of Langroods Farm. I can see it now; the letter was in a dark blue envelope and caused considerable excitement and discussion. Thereafter we moved to Langroods Farm a little further up the hill towards High Bradley.

High Bradley was a hamlet of a very few largely period houses sheltered beneath the moor. Here lived my paternal grandparents who had retired from farming. My uncle still lived there, in the house in which he was born, and even my mother had once lived at High Bradley at the Old Hall Farm. Father was a member of the Throup family. We were able to trace his family back in direct male line for six centuries without a gap, which is quite an achievement for an ordinary family. I expected that they would all have been farmers or farm labourers, but not so. It turned out that they had been closely connected with the Church and performed many services that civil servants do today. They had even been the pursuivants largely responsible for rounding up the Pilgrim Fathers, as they eventually became known, in Nottinghamshire, resulting in their epic voyage to America on the Mayflower.

My grandparents' old cottage had once apparently been two cottages as it still had two front doors and two staircases, but there was no running water. When they retired from farming they wanted to continue living at High Bradley and were fortunate in being able to find a vacant property where location mattered

6

more than the mod-cons of the day. The old house was reputed to have once been a pub known as the Drovers' Arms and still generated the aura of a bygone era.

The old couple lived to be 89 and 92 years of age and were ably looked after by their daughter, my Auntie Anice. Grandma was stone deaf and to communicate at all we had to shout at the tops of our voices down an ear trumpet. Grandfather, on the other hand, seemed blessed with reasonable hearing, but he was almost blind as the result of a botched cataract operation and had to grope his way from room to room. He wore an old frock coat with two buttons and pleats down the back. It was green with age and probably the same coat in which he had had his photograph taken as a young man. He also had a striped jacket which was handed down to my father on grandfather's demise. My father wore this around the house and always referred to it jokingly as his 'legacy'.

Grandma always wore a floor-length dress, usually of black satin with a bunch of lace at her throat. Nobody ever saw her ankles for she also wore high buttoned-up boots which had to be laboriously fastened each day with a purpose-built button hook — all relics of the Victorian era, I suppose.

Once, in old age, Grandma had a query. Referring to my Grandfather she said, "Who is that old chap sitting in the corner? He never gets to any work". My auntie laughed. "Why, that's your loving husband!" she replied with a twinkle in

her eye, but Grandma was not impressed. "Nay, never," she said, "I never married an old cove like yon!"

Grandma had come from Morecambe as a young girl to work in Skipton and later on a farm at Snaygill, near Bradley. Her name was Fanny Woodhouse and she belonged to an old Morecambe fishing family. The Woodhouse family was one of four families which had supposedly founded Morecambe, originally a small fishing village called Poulton. It only became known as Morecambe in the late eighteen hundreds and grew in size as a holiday resort when workers in the mills flooded in for their annual holidays. Later, the Woodhouse family took advantage of the new opportunities and many family members were to be found running wet fish shops, boarding houses and even large hotels. Different brothers of the Woodhouse family had various trades and they ran the only Post Office in the Poulton area at that time. Grandma's cousin, William Woodhouse, even became a celebrated artist exhibiting his work at the Royal Academy, the Royal Scottish Academy and elsewhere. The family's main involvement, however, was in fishing. They owned their family boats; in winter fishing from the bay, but in summer they often diversified and took visitors for a sail around the bay at a shilling a time.

A Morecambe fishing boat

Once, when on a day out, we pottered out our shilling for the trip round the bay. My brother, then a small boy, was sitting at one end of the boat, fiddling around with some ropes which didn't seem to be serving any useful purpose. Suddenly the heavy wooden mast fell down and the boat tipped ominously to one side. My father's cousin, Tom, who was sailing the boat, rushed across and rectified matters or we would all have ended up in a watery grave in Morecambe Bay.

Sadly, a few members of the Woodhouse family including one of Grandma's brothers and her nephew were drowned at sea and I was told that not one of the fishermen could swim. Grandma's sister, Emma, had a strange experience. One wild and stormy night her sons went out fishing as usual. She awoke at around three o'clock in the morning and said that she had heard Ralph calling 'Mother' three times. Next day he did not return, but his body was washed up three weeks later at Blackpool.

The weather dominated the lives of fishermen. If one fisherman met another in the street, a comment would always be made about the weather, such as "The wind's blowing nicely over the wah-tah." As a young man my father would sometimes go to visit his Morecambe relations. It always amused him that when he was returning to the station to board the train they would express the hope that he would have 'a fair wind' on his return journey.

Moor Cottage, High Bradley

MEL

In the windswept north country,
Sheltered from the moor,
The cottage viewed with ageless calm
The valley spread before.
The weathered walls in rough-hewn stone
Absorbed the landscape round,
About that childhood anchorage
No jarring note was found.

A wooden door set in the wall
Gained eager access to
A grassy orchard, where at times
The billowing washing blew.
Old-fashioned flowers in a strip
Of garden bloomed each year,
Across the path, a deep-set well,
With water, crystal clear.

Within, some aura lingered on,
Of days forgotten, when
As hostelry, 'The Drovers' Arms',
It served the droving men.
Of men who, gathering round the fire,
Sought refuge from the cold,
Quaffed home-brewed ale, blew curling smoke,
And many a good tale told.

The stone-flagged kitchen floor
Inclined from south to north, so that
The northern table legs were sawn
To make the surface flat!
On mullioned window sills there bloomed
Geraniums, scarlet, green,
While on a board nearby, there stood
Two pails of water, clean.

And still the pictures on the wall
Before my mind's eye pass,
A Bible scene in black and red,
Hand-painted on to glass.

A print from some old magazine,
Now honoured, framed instead,
'Fixed by grandma. Can't get out,'
The amusing caption said.

Who painted 'Lady X' in oils?
Who was she? What her name?
(The artist's signature cut off
Long since, to fit the frame!)
This, of a pair, alone survived,
But whom did they denote?
(The other canvas used with thrift,
Way back, to caulk a boat!)

Behind my Grandpapa's long couch —
Treasure for childish eyes!
A wooden screen, excluding draughts,
Yet filled with gay surprise.
Adorned with countless coloured scraps —
A young child's heart's beguiler,
From posies, pixies, fairy folk
To Samson and Delilah.

Or to the parlour we withdrew,
With china cups for tea,
To hear but the ticking of a clock
Brings it back to me.
Lit by the lamplight's mellow glow,
The cares of day were shed
As dancing firelight leaped
To tinge the rafters overhead.

And skilful hands had worked to style
The fire's red wood surround
From grandma's old four-poster bed —
Once curtains hung around.
Of silk they were, an odd design,
I gazed in awe-struck hush
At patterned Moses, patterned flames
Before the Burning Bush.

A candle lit the way upstairs
With shadowy, plunging beams.
Poor children of today's harsh glare,
There is no room for dreams.

12

LIFE ON THE FARM

13

We children had a happy life on the farm. In common with everybody else at the time we never missed the mod-cons we never had because we knew no other. There was no such thing as central heating, but we did have a gas light in the house. The ceilings were very low and once Doctor MacLeod (whose son became Chancellor of the Exchequer) swiped off all the delicate gas mantles with the top of his head.

In the kitchen there was a cold water tap which ran on to a stone sink. Hot water was obtained by filling up a tank by the side of the coal fire, known as the boiler. There was no bathroom, but we had a bath in a tin bath placed in front of the fire every Friday night. The 'toilet' was outside, across a small croft next to the pig sty.

We always had a good fire, but the heat generated did not seem to permeate the bedrooms. In frosty weather we would waken to the sight of the ice on the inside of the windows having formed delicate swirling patterns of ferns and fronds; an artist could not have done better. There were no tractors then, but we had two farm horses, Kitty and Papyrus, and now and again father would pull one of us up behind him and we would gallop with gay abandon on horseback down the front meadow.

Father and his man got up at about half past four in the morning to hand-milk the cows. There was no electricity in the shippons, but dad had a paraffin storm lamp which he moved from nail to nail on the whitewashed walls as he progressed from cow to cow.

14

At one time tuberculosis was rife among dairy cattle. Sometimes father would notice that a certain cow, for instance, was going very thin, or 'going to a screw' as he called it. This was probably a cow infected with tuberculosis, but there was then no means of testing and the milk from the infected cow was poured in with all the rest and we were drinking it along with everybody else.

The morning's milk having been cooled and filtered was contained in big milk kits, holding about twelve gallons each, which were transported by horse and float to catch the 7:30 am train from Skipton to Leeds, where it was collected by a private milk retailer whose job it was to deliver it to his customers on the streets of Leeds. This was not without its traumas. There was no Milk Marketing Board in those days and the farmer had to sort out any problems himself. Sometimes the customer in Leeds did not pay and we looked anxiously for the arrival of the postman each morning when payment was due. Once my father went to Leeds chasing the money, but a maid answered the door and said that her employer was away on holiday in the south of France!

It was even worse when the Leeds man gave a week's notice, which fortunately did not happen often. It meant that at the end of the week there was no money coming in. The cows appeared as usual to be milked, but there was nowhere for the milk to go and the farmer had to feed, not only his family, but all his farm stock as well. When this happened, Dad had to go by train from Skipton and tramp the unfamiliar streets of Leeds trying to find another outlet for his milk.

In the meantime, the solution was to make butter. Out would come the hand-operated separator to separate the cream from the milk, the separated milk being fed to the pigs. The cream was poured into a wooden churn and then began the arduous task of churning by turning a handle which agitated the cream by means of paddles inside. This was anything but simple. Sometimes, if we were lucky, the churning time would be relatively short, but in cold weather the process could take hours. Churning seemed to go for ever and everyone had to give a hand. After what seemed an eternity the cream inside became thicker and harder to work, and then, "oh joy!" a swishing sound could be heard from within and we knew that, at last, the cream had 'cracked' as the separation was called. When the lid was removed little globules of butter could be seen floating about in a sea of buttermilk.

The sour buttermilk was then poured off and fed to the pigs. The globules were then gathered together and placed in a wooden butter bowl which mother had previously scalded out and rinsed with cold water to avoid the contents sticking.

Mother then kneaded the butter with her hands which forced out the buttermilk. The butter bowl was filled up time and again with cold water and the cloudy water poured off. When the water was clear she knew that the butter left would be sweet and not rancid or streaky as some farmers' butter could be. Lastly, she threw in a handful of salt, weighed the butter, shaped it with butter pats, wrapped it in grease-proof paper and it was ready for sale. It was then my job, as a child, to hawk the butter around the village, but once the butter had been tasted there was no problem with selling it.

After a few weeks, another customer in Leeds would be found and the butter making would thankfully be abandoned. Bear in mind that there was no dole for a self-employed man who had to sink or swim by his own efforts.

Lambing time was a landmark in the farming year. Sometimes the farmer or his family had to sit up all night with an old Tilley Lamp, ready to go out and attend to a lambing sheep if there was an emergency, or sometimes in the middle of the night new born lambs would be brought into the house to recover from the cold by the open fire.

Another memorable time was haytime, which depended so much on the vagaries of our English weather. An Irishman would be hired for a month to help with the excessive workload, but sometimes in wet weather we were no further at the end of the month than we had been at the beginning. We children were roped in to help of course, our job being mainly to trample down the hay on the 'moo' (the hay loft), so making room for more. As the 'moo' rose so did we, until our heads were scraping the cobwebbed slates undisturbed from the year before. But there were compensations, such as the 'drinking' times when we all relaxed for a welcome break, drinking ginger beer, eating sandwiches and generally jollying one another along.

The farm man in those days worked long hours whenever he was required, including Saturday mornings, and all for £1 a week and his 'keep' which was the standard wage at that time. Once, our farm man asked my father if he could have Saturday morning off. Initially my dad refused his request as there was work to be done, but the man remonstrated "I shall 'av to 'av it off, boss; I'm getting wed!".

Pig killing was another landmark event. The slaughter usually took place outside in the yard but when this was due to happen I usually managed to plead that my presence was needed elsewhere.

It was said that every part of the pig could be used, except the grunt. The animal's carcase was hung up to drain and then salted on large horizontal stone slabs in the farmhouse pantry. The fat-bearing 'leaves' were rendered down in a hot oven, producing drip-white lard and delicious 'cracklings' when the fat had been run off. There was plenty of spare-rib and bacon, and even the bladder could be blown up and used as a football.

How fortunate we were as children to have access to open spaces and beautiful countryside. By the side of the farmhouse was an orchard where we grew cherries, apples, pears and plums. There was even an enormous walnut tree at the bottom of the garden. We climbed over a stile in the orchard into the meadow and across the meadow to Pith Hill Wood, where we picked bluebells, marsh marigolds and celandines to our hearts' content. My father loved this wood with its abundance of wildlife, and to him it was always the 'Enchanted Wood'.

The Range

The pre-war old-fashioned ranges were hard work, but had much to commend them, True, they had to be black-leaded, and the ashes cleaned out every day with a 'cowl-rake', but the open fire was warm and welcoming, and countless scraps were disposed of in the flames without creating overflowing dustbin problems.

The fireside was where all the household action took place. Plates stood warming on the hearth, the kettle sang on the hob and potatoes boiled in iron pans on the grate. Dough was set to rise before the fire in large yellow-enamelled bowls, and the delicious smell of baking pervaded the house as apple-pies cooked in the side oven, or parkins cooled in their tins. There were no knobs to twiddle to regulate the heat but somehow we managed.

On wet Mondays, however, the clothes horse took priority and flat irons were heated alternately on the glowing embers.

With only a cold water tap on to a stone slopstone, the fireside 'boiler' was indispensable. Cold water was tipped in from a pail to the fireside tank, and warm water, when needed, ladled out with a lading can.

If the fire roared away too quickly, Grandma (with a mind to the next coal bill) had ready large balls of crumpled newspaper soaked in cold water which were placed strategically among the flames. These were the 'slackeners', and the old-fashioned answer to present-day push-button control.

THE QUARRY

My maternal Grandfather, Ambrose, also a farmer, moved to Bradley from Wigglesworth. He had married Sarah Elton, a farmer's daughter from Rochdale, who had strayed from her native environment to take up a teaching appointment at Ribchester. At the time of her marriage she was headteacher of the small village school at Marton. Later in life she suffered from rheumatic fever, supposedly caused through sleeping in damp beds at college. She died when Ambrose was only about forty five, but he never married again, living instead with Annie, the middle of his three daughters.

Annie had married Harry Raw who had left Pateley Bridge to work in the quarry at Bradley. His relations all lived around the Pateley area and this is where the connection with Ripon began. Harry's family had owned their own stonemason's business but when the business folded he came to Bradley to work in the quarry, this being work with which he was familiar.

Bradley Quarry was known for producing high-quality stone and several men were employed, but by the time Harry arrived it was almost worked-out and not long afterwards ceased producing stone on a commercial basis. Grandfather Ambrose then bought the worked-out quarry or 'delph', as it was sometimes called, and subsequently the family had a house built on quarry land at Ryefield.

This quarry afforded Uncle Harry with the opportunity to exercise his stonemason's skills when he felt like it as there was still plenty of stone lying around, but the quarry was no longer viable as a commercial enterprise. Eventually my father too had a house built from this stone at Overton Crofts half way up to High Bradley. In addition, Harry turned every bit of flat land in the quarry into hen pens and so was able to make a living without going off the premises to work.

In this worked-out quarry my cousin Gladys, my brother Leonard and I, spent many happy hours. There were little humps and hills all over the place, with rocks to climb and many secret little places in which to construct our dens.

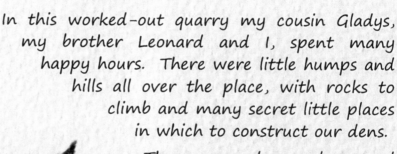

There was also a deep and rather menacing waterhole beneath the rock face but we skirted around it, giving it as wide a berth as possible in case we slipped and ended up in the murky green depths.

The quarry proliferated with wild flowers. In spring the pens were carpeted with bluebells. I can remember once, when I must have been very young, carefully stripping off the petals of a bluebell, hoping — just hoping — that I might find a fairy inside. Foxgloves grew in abundance among the piles of stones, and in the backend of the year luscious blackberries ran riot, which we were able to pick to our hearts' content without competition since this was private ground. No doubt this was also the reason why we usually got first prize for the best vase of wild flowers at the local show.

Meanwhile Harry settled down well in Bradley. Sometimes he worked the stone himself when stone was required and I used to watch him splitting a huge rock by inserting a wedge in an existing crack and marvelled how effective a simple hammer and wedge could be. He always kept in touch with his relations from the Pateley area, particularly his sister Hetty, who had married and lived in Lickley Street, Ripon, our later holiday destination.

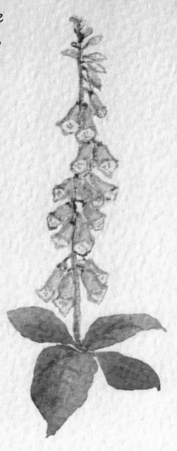

THE JOURNEY

Somewhere along the line someone came up with the idea that it would be good for my cousin, Gladys, if I went with her for company when she went to stay with her Aunt Hetty and Uncle Jack in Ripon, and naturally I jumped at the chance.

I knew nothing about towns and had hardly ever had a night away from my home village. I was used to old houses with beamed ceilings, mullioned windows and geraniums on the windowsills. Indeed, as a child, I realised that the houses my relations lived in were somehow 'different' and I remember thinking, 'Why can't I live in a house in a street like most of my school friends?' Now I was about to live the experience.

Arrangements were made and at long last the awaited day of departure came. With great excitement we piled into the old Trojan car driven by Uncle Harry. There were not that many vehicles on the road at that time and a car journey was still an exciting adventure.

We chugged slowly along, fifteen miles to the hour
In an old Trojan car – quite a feat.
Over Blubberhouse Moor, we hardly dare breathe
And clung to the sides of our seat.

The route took us through Skipton and over Blubberhouses Moor. This was the first of a few annual journeys and certain features along the way became landmarks to look out for each year. After chugging along at all of about fifteen miles per hour we began the long descent from Blubberhouses. Huge rocks stood sentinel over the scene. They look the same today as they looked all those years ago and will remain unchanged for years to come. One slight difference is that mobile phone masts have sprung up in the background reminding us of the so-called march of progress.

Rocks on the moor like sentinels stood
Brooding, bold, rugged and grey.
Tomorrow, they will have the same
Dark outline as today.

27

The hair-raising bit came next, as with our hearts in our mouths we negotiated the 'ravine' — a steep drop on the passenger side.   Looking at it now, I wonder why we were so terrified, but in those days we felt to be taking our lives in our hands.

Across from the road, on the side of the moor, was a ruined farm. When the house was last occupied I do not know, but it must have been a long time ago as it was almost as ruined then as it is today. Even today this old farmstead intrigues me.

A ruined homestead, once a farm,
Which nature could not foil,
For still green fields midst bog and moor
Bear witness to man's toil.

Before the days of mechanical help, some poor husbandman must have toiled long and hard to create a small farm from the inhospitable moorland — a farm big enough to support a family. He had picked up large stones and used them to wall off small fields and he had cultivated the ground. Little paths radiated from the farmhouse and I imagine him returning to his family in the now tumble-down farmhouse or keeper's cottage after hours of toil. The land is surrounded by moorland but it is still a little green oasis among the rough ground, bearing witness to the struggles of a bygone age. I can imagine the candle or lamp-light shining out on this bleak hillside in the darkness and I people the dwelling in my mind's eye as I pass.

Gradually the moorland gave way to green fields. It is strange what unimportant images remain locked in the memory. There was a working farm by the roadside. Outside the door stood a Victorian chair with a horsehair seat and on the seat was placed a bowl of eggs, presumably advertising the fact to passers-by that free range eggs were for sale. (Well, they were all free range in those days.) Every year we looked out for the chair and eggs which became part of the magic of the journey and the eggs were always there. Of course we never stopped to buy any because we had hens of our own.

How excited we were as we neared the old city,

Joy knew no bounds and our restlessness grew,

"I can see Ripon Minster", we shouted at last,

As round the next corner it came into view.

Still we chugged along. Then, unexpectedly, we turned a corner and Ripon Minster came into view across the fields. How thrilled we were! There were excited cries of, "I can see t'Minster", and we knew that our journey was reaching its end. Each year, therefore, it became a sort of competition to see who could be the first to spot the Cathedral.

**Approach
to Ripon**

LOW SKELLGATE
CLOSE

The Obelisk in the
Market Square can
be seen rising above
the roof tops.

31

MEL

Eventually the bridge over the Skell and the imposing office frontage of Williamson's varnish works came into view, indicating that we had passed the outskirts of the city. As we climbed up narrow Low Skellgate towards the Market Square I noticed that old cottages by the roadside still had their old wooden shutters. The renovated cottages are still there but the shutters have gone. We drove alongside the Market Square and turned right down Allhallowgate and along Priest Lane, until finally turning a sharp left. Lickley Street, built on a sizeable slope, opened up before us, with number twenty-six, the house of our hosts, situated on the left at the bottom of the hill.

Old cottages down Skellgate way
Were lit by candle light.
As evening shadows fell
They closed the shutters for the night.

LICKLEY STREET

33

Lickley Street was not the grandest street in the world, but it had everything that one expected at the time, and I thought it was wonderful. Perhaps my enchantment with it owed as much to the warm welcome we received as to bricks and mortar. Compared with many Victorian dwellings of that era it afforded many amenities not then in general usage with enough space to bring up a family.

I do not know how many houses there were in this very long and hilly street but it was relatively quiet as it was not a through road. Although the houses were all joined together in a long line, some blocks seemed to have been built slightly differently from the others and probably at different times. The fronts of the houses opened directly on to the street from a small front room, but there were long gardens at the back on our side of the road where we could enjoy the open air and watch the sunsets.

Long years have passed and I've travelled far,
With Petra or Rome at my feet,
But nothing surpasses those halcyon days
Of my childhood, down long Lickley Street.

The long garden at the back of number twenty-six was kept neat and tidy with room for flowers and a few vegetables. Since Jack and Hetty were particularly friendly with their neighbours next door on one side, the fence between the two had been adapted for use. A few feet had been removed from the very top of the fence and had been replaced with a horizontal piece of wood which served as a seat, so that on summer evenings neighbours could enjoy one another's company from either side by literally sitting on the fence.

A broad unpaved walkway ran along the top of the gardens and disappeared through an archway giving access to the front street. At the other side of the walkway at the top of the garden at number twenty-six was a brick building, and round the end of the building were the outside toilets, one for each family.

This might hardly seem to be worthy of mention but even in the 1930s there were still properties around the Skipton area where two or more families shared outside conveniences.

A high wall divided the Lickley Street property from what lay beyond and occasionally our curiosity got the better of us as we scaled the wall to peep over. There appeared to be a large area of waste ground on the other side, where the fire station now is. Maybe it had once been a garden as a pear tree hung over the wall. In the aforementioned brick building Jack kept a pig. In fact, many householders kept a pig in those days, if they had enough space, as pigs were considered to be a natural method of recycling (a process which causes us to have so many headaches today). No doubt this would not be allowed nowadays, what with 'Health and Safety' and all that, but I do not remember any unsavoury smells or piggy noises emanating from the building. When the time came I expect the pig would emerge into the daylight to meet its fate and to be replaced with a younger version. It could not have been a very happy life for the solitary pig, but keeping a pig was acceptable at the time and would have provided a little bit of extra income.

The air whistled past
As we soared high and free
On a swing in the park
Beneath this tall tree.

I REMEMBER,
I REMEMBER

I remember, I remember
Where I was used to swing,
And thought the air must rush as fresh
To swallows on the wing.
My spirit flew in feathers then,
That is so heavy now,
And summer pools could hardly cool
The fever on my brow!

Thomas Hood
(extract)

What really for me got Lickley Street a five-star rating was the park at the end of the street. A small gate led directly into the park which was an open grassy area with sturdy swings and a see-saw. For Gladys and me the star attraction was the swing erected on a slight rise beneath a tall tree and within sight of the front door. We played for hours on this swing which had solid metal rods as side supports rather than the usual floppy chains. By bending our knees at the appropriate time we were able to soar higher and higher, at the same time getting a bird's eye view of what was going on around. One time we could see new houses being built in the direction of Fishergreen. Unusually they seemed to be almost Dutch in shape and I seem to remember that they were painted in pastel colours. Now after such a short time these houses appear almost deserted and unloved.

In those days Lickley Street children could be packed off to the park to play in perfect safety because of the direct access. This is possible no more. A fairly busy road connecting the bypass to the City centre runs across the bottom of the street and now children have to look both ways before crossing into the park.

The word soon got around that two strange children were staying with Jack and Hetty and we were not short of friendly playmates gathering round, eager to make the acquaintance of these strangers who could have been from outer space. Playmates included the Hawksworth children, Harry and Aggie, who lived a couple of doors away, Cyril Lancaster (no relation to me) and occasionally Mabel Dunning from the top shop, which has since been converted into a house. These Lickley Street children always seemed to remember us well enough from the year before and when we returned each August we all effortlessly picked up the threads.

Another bonus for us was that Ripon's historical horn blower, then Mr Blackburn, lived just across the street. Every evening approaching nine o'clock he would sally forth dressed in his uniform and carrying his impressively curved horn. Soon, onlookers would gather round as he sounded the horn at the four corners of the Obelisk in the Market Square, but he was such a common sight in Lickley Street that to the local children playing about he hardly merited a second glance.

Across the road from the top of Lickley Street stood the Cathedral Boys' School which was pulled down in 1962. A little further away, where Priest Lane joins Allhallowgate, was a fish and chip shop. I particularly remember this shop because the proprietor immediately spotted that I was a stranger and asked me where I came from. When I told him that I was from a village called Bradley at the other side of Skipton he became immediately interested and asked me if I knew Johnny Clay who happened to be the landlord of the Slaters' Arms there. It truly is a small world.

The Hornblower lived across the street
And every night at nine
He sallied forth to sound his horn,
The weather wet or shine.

The Hornblower

In earlier times there was a connection between the office of Wakeman and the Hornblower since the Wakeman's stint of duty lasted from 9 o'clock in the evening, when the Hornblower sounded his horn, until dawn.

The Hornblower still blows his horn at 9 o'clock at the four corners of the Obelisk in the Market Square, but no one knows when the custom first began. People in the medieval period were supposed to remain indoors during the hours of darkness and the curfew was also a precaution against fire (the word curfew itself being derived from the French 'couvre feu', or 'cover the fire').

The Hornblower wears a black tricorne hat and a coat trimmed with red and he can be sure of a few curious spectators gathering round, particularly on a summer's evening when his presence projects a little glimpse of former times on to present-day Ripon.

LICKLEY STREET DAYS

Stepping stones across the River Skell

We walked by the river
In Ure's evening sheen
To the banks of the Skell
And along Fishergreen.

We leaped across the stepping stones
Set in the river's flow,
And tried to keep upon our feet
As fishes swam below.

Jack and Hetty had no children but we got the impression that they enjoyed having us just as much as we enjoyed being there. I don't suppose that a childless couple bordering on middle age were exactly ecstatic about fishing for tiddlers, but they appeared to be, thus making our excursions to Fishergreen all the more enjoyable. Inevitably we returned with our trophies of a few tiddlers which we proudly displayed in jam jars on the kitchen window sill for the rest of the week. I have since wondered what those poor little fish had done to be condemned to swim endlessly round in a glass prison until meeting an untimely end.

The stepping stones across the Skell at Fishergreen were an added attraction and we never tired of leaping fearlessly across from stone to stone without slipping or getting our feet wet. Perhaps there was less pollution in those days but there seemed to be a fair number of sizeable fish swimming around in the clear waters. Fishergreen hardly seems recognisable to me now that modern houses have been built there.

There was no television in those days and no computer games, but on summer evenings we went for long walks or on rainy days amused ourselves playing board games in front of an open fire.

Jack and Hetty were friendly with someone who lived at the top of the street on the other side which is now only an open space. One evening this neighbour came down with a planchette to amuse us. I had not seen one before nor have I seen one since. It was a small flat board with two little wheels at the back on which two people rested their hands. A pencil was pushed through a hole at the front. As far as I remember she asked this contraption a question and it responded by writing an answer. The planchette wrote at such a speed that she had continually to feed it with new sheets of paper or it would have continued writing on the table. It was all a bit spooky. I am certain that nobody could have pushed it or guided it in any way, and can only think that it worked because of something to do with the subconscious mind. Anyway, the diversion passed an hour or two.

One year when we visited Lickley Street there must have been a recession and workers were being laid off seemingly in droves at Williamson's varnish works where Jack was employed. I have never forgotten how each day he came home with a long face announcing gloomily that 'X number of men were laid off today' and it seemed to be only a matter of time before his turn came. He did survive longer than most, but inevitably the blow fell. Finding new work was not easy but eventually I heard that he had managed to secure a job as a guard in a bank and this kept the wolf from the door until his retirement, as far as I know. To be witness to someone in daily fear of losing his job was a new experience for me as the fear of unemployment was not a situation that faced my farming relations. However, on reflection, when I thought back to the butter-making days with no unemployment pay to fall back on, I decided that there was nothing much to choose between either situation.

Sometimes Jack and Hetty would invite their nephew, Willie, and his wife Doris, from Pateley, to come and stay while we were there on the principle of 'the more the merrier' and they always accepted me as though I were one of the family. Willie's upbringing had been somewhat unconventional. His father Jimmy was Hetty's brother and when Jimmy's wife died in childbirth when their son was born he was so distraught that he emigrated to Australia, leaving the small baby to be brought up by the step-grandmother. Hence, Willie never knew his father, but he had never known any other life and so accepted what seemed an odd situation without question. Jimmy meanwhile went on to make a new life for himself in Australia, never marrying again but working out in the Bush and eking out a living as a small farmer. The family kept in touch and from time to time presents would arrive from Australia. I particularly remember decorative ostrich eggs displayed under a glass dome arriving at Uncle Harry's. These were proudly displayed on the sideboard for many years until inevitably they eventually went out of fashion and were then relegated to a storage cupboard.

When Willie was middle-aged a unique opportunity to speak to the father he had never known presented itself. Willie won a newspaper competition with an unusual prize. He was taken to a recording studio in Leeds and at the same time his father was brought down from the Bush and taken to a recording studio in Australia. The two were then able to converse and perhaps make up a little for lost time. At any rate it seemed to afford the abandoned son a lot of pleasure.

Jimmy never found the pot of gold at the end of the Australian rainbow (even supposing he wanted to). Many many years later, when the participants had passed away, Gladys's daughter went to Australia for a holiday with the added incentive of trying to find something of her great-uncle's whereabouts. Not only did she track down where he had lived but also managed to find the remains of his house and someone who actually remembered the old man, hence it proved to be a most satisfying experience.

The Minster crowns the roof tops
In sun or winter snow,
Conveys a sense of timelessness
As centuries come and go.

SAINT WILFRID

I suspect that we were invited to Ripon especially in August because it was thought that we would enjoy the annual procession in honour of Saint Wilfrid and the events associated with it. They were right. It was with mounting excitement that we joined the crowds lining the roads when, leading the procession, 'Daddy Wilfra' came into view sitting astride a white horse. It is amazing to think that after hundreds of years interrupted by two World Wars, Saint Wilfrid is still remembered in this way. The rest of the colourful procession followed, but that was not the end of the commemoration. At night the celebrations were continued at the fun-fair in the Market Place, when amid the noise and the blaring music we enjoyed the stalls, the roundabouts, the bumper cars and everything else a fair had to offer. I was disappointed later that for a time the fair ceased to be held in the Market Place, which as a child had seemed an ideal venue to me, but no doubt residents at the Unicorn Hotel on the Square would view it differently. I believe that the fair has since been reinstated in the Market Place.

With excitement we waited beneath summer's sky,
'Daddy Wilfra' himself, then on horseback rode by.

Who was Wilfrid?

The real Wilfrid was far removed from the cosy Santa Clausy image I had as a child of a benign elderly gentleman riding about on a white horse. The real Wilfrid was born in 634 AD to a noble Northumbrian Christian family. At that time England was still divided into kingdoms. Wilfrid's family was well connected and knew all the right people, hence Wilfrid had opportunities denied to many people.

At the age of fourteen Wilfrid was sent to Lindisfarne, otherwise known as Holy Island, to care for a dying nobleman in the monastery there. He left Lindisfarne determined to become a monk, but first he wanted to visit Rome, the centre of the Christian faith. This he did, but it was a dangerous journey without maps or calendars. Roads were rough tracks, often through forests where wild animals roamed at will. How did he and his companions find their way? They must have had a system of guides familiar with their own area who escorted them from place to place.

When Wilfrid returned he was full of enthusiasm for Roman architecture and culture, and he imported European craftsmen to help him to realise his dream of erecting fine buildings in England also. After returning in 661 AD he was granted the monastery at Ripon which the then occupants had to vacate to accommodate him. He ruled wisely as abbot for three years and worked hard to introduce Roman rules. At that time there were differences between the Roman Church and the existing Celtic Church largely run by Irish monks. The Synod of Whitby in 664 AD was set up to resolve these differences. Wilfrid spoke up so eloquently for the Roman Church that matters were found in their favour.

(Continued over)

Wilfrid was now riding high and nominated to the bishopric of Northumberland and he chose to go to Compiègne, France, to be consecrated. He loved the pomp and ceremony of the Roman Church and spent money lavishly. It is said that he was carried into the cathedral there seated on a golden throne attended by no fewer than nine bishops.

He returned to Ripon and erected an entirely new church in the Roman manner and founded an abbey at Hexham. In later years these churches and replacement churches are believed to have been destroyed, firstly by the Danes and afterwards by the Normans during the 'Harrying of the North'. Being deep underground, the crypts only have survived and the crypt at Ripon is situated beneath the High Altar of the present Minster which was built by Bishop Roger.

Wilfrid became Bishop of York and Hexham but was never Bishop of Ripon. Nevertheless, Ripon was his favourite place and it was to Ripon that he came when beset by troubles. He was very outspoken and a volatile character who had an unfortunate knack of upsetting his superiors. From time to time he was banished – even imprisoned – reinstated and banished again. His wealth and importance sometimes made him the subject of envy, but wherever possible he continued to found churches. He spent some time doing missionary work in Sussex, at that time untouched by Christianity. It his said that his private life was disciplined, simple and restrained. His later years were spent in trying to assert his rights and he went twice more to Rome to petition the Pope, the last time when he was already an old man.

Wilfrid worked hard to put Christianity on a firm foundation in England and for this the Christian Church owes him a debt of gratitude. He was taken ill when visiting the monastery at Oundle, Northamptonshire and died there at the age of seventy five. According to an earlier request his body was transported to his beloved Ripon for burial, but its whereabouts have been lost.

WILFRA TARTS

8oz shortcrust pastry
½ pint milk
1oz white breadcrumbs
4oz butter
2oz ground almonds
1oz caster sugar
Grated rind of lemon
3 eggs

Roll the pastry thinly and
cut out tartlet cases.

Boil the milk and
add the breadcrumbs.

Cool for 20 minutes until the
breadcrumbs have soaked up the milk.

Stir in the butter, ground almonds,
sugar and grated lemon rind.

Beat the eggs and add one by one.

Fill each tart with mixture.

Bake for 20 minutes at 375°F.

'Wilfra' Tarts

Naturally, all kinds of customs and traditions grew up around the Feast of St Wilfrid and in recent times 'Wilfra' tarts, spice bread or apple pie with cheese, would be placed outside houses for passers-by on the processional route.

This recipe makes about 24 tarts.

The taste can be pepped up if a little jam is spooned into the base of the pastry cases.

And then, once a year, noise and fun filled the Square
As the Market Place throbbed to the sound of the fair.

MEL
51

The Fairground

MEL

Canned pop music, loudly blaring,
Shattering the evening air,
Calls the young ones to be sharing
All the hotch-potch of the fair.
Gaudy lights in red and yellow
Flash their message in the sky,
Hear the showmen bawl and bellow
Through the mike, at passers by.
Gangling long-haired youths escorting
Giggling girls with eyes like stars,
By the scaffolding, supporting
Noah's Arks and bumper cars.
Faster, faster, onward whirling
Colours blended into one,
Screaming, shouting, twisting, twirling,
Attributes of having fun.

"See the side-shows — just a tanner,
Freaks and what the butler spied,"
On the crowd goes, surging, milling,
Thrills, excitements side-by-side.
"Bingo tickets? Take a pot-shot?
Try your luck, Sir. Have a toss.
Win a coconut, or why not
Toffee apples or candyfloss?"
See the women, loud, gum chewing,
Hugging outsize cuddly toys,
Watch your pockets! Trouble brewing
From slick, slight-of-handsome boys!
Spotty youths, impressing girl-friends,
Ring the bell to test their strength,
Fathers dragging tired toddlers
Carry goldfish home at length.

THE CATHEDRAL

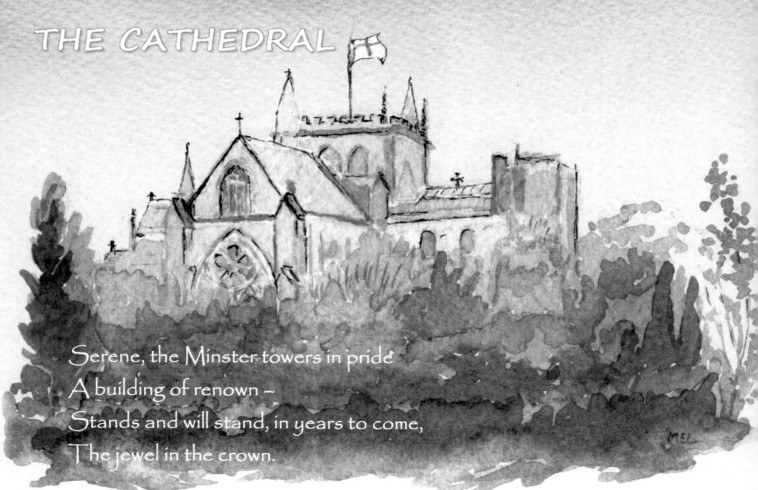

Serene, the Minster towers in pride
A building of renown –
Stands and will stand, in years to come,
The jewel in the crown.

Our annual visit to Ripon would not have been complete without a glimpse inside the Cathedral. As a child I marvelled at the towering stone columns and the general feeling of space and wondered how the medieval builders had achieved so much without the aid of modern technology. I cannot remember much detail about the Minster as a child, except, as I say, giving the impression of spaciousness and grandeur.

In later years I was fortunate in being able to visit the Middle East several times, and naturally I visited the beautiful temples and mosques of Jerusalem. To enter The Dome of The Rock we were required to remove our shoes, which we left under cover some distance away and this necessitated walking quite a way in the open air. It was the year of the big snow and I remember thinking that when we planned our visit I had not bargained for a walk across the snow in bare feet in Jerusalem! Anybody at home would have thought that we were mad! The mosques were splendidly different from English architecture and I remember comparing them in my mind's eye with our English cathedrals which I had not visited for some time. A while later I again visited Ripon Cathedral, and as I stood inside near the back I remember thinking 'Our English architecture could perhaps be equalled, but never surpassed'.

THE MINSTER THROUGH THE YEARS

In 1836 Ripon Minster became the Cathedral Church of Saint Peter and Saint Wilfrid, and the fact that it survived is a testimony to the unquenchable human spirit. An early church on the site was built about 655 AD by Saint Wilfrid, with whom Ripon is ever associated. All that survives, however, is the Saxon crypt, reputably once under the high altar of Wilfrid's church. This early church was probably destroyed by the Danes. A replacement church also suffered the same fate, this time destroyed by the Normans during the 'Harrying of the North' when William the Conqueror ravaged the northern counties in order to beat them into submission in the eleventh century.

The Normans, however, having achieved their aim, then tried to make amends, and in 1154, soon after the Norman Conquest, the building of the present Cathedral began to take its early shape, at the instigation of a Norman, Archbishop Roger Pont l'Evesque.

Roger built for posterity, knowing that such a monumental work would extend far beyond his lifetime, and when he died in 1181 there was understandably much work to be done.

In 1220 Archbishop de Grey built the present familiar early English west front and twin towers surmounted by wooden spires covered with lead, which gave extra height above the rather squat stone towers.

The story of the Cathedral through the centuries is a story of constant neglect, repair and rebuilding. Not only did those responsible for its upkeep have to contend with the vagaries of the weather but also much depended upon the capabilities or inadequacies of the human beings in charge. Moreover, national emergencies played a part. In the 13th and 14th centuries the Scots, buoyed up by their victory over the English at Bannockburn, came continually over the Border wreaking havoc on the way. The year 1318 was a particularly dangerous time. The Scots had already done their worst at Northallerton and Boroughbridge and when they reached Ripon the townspeople fled in terror to the Minster which they had fortified and which they managed to hold for three days. On payment of a ransom the Minster was largely spared, but as with appeasement generally the Scots came back for more the following year and much damage was done. The onset of the Black Death halted the restoration process as some workmen refused to enter the town for fear of contamination. Maintenance work was neglected and circa 1450 the corner of the central tower collapsed into the roof and for some years the Minster was unusable. In 1534 came that landmark in English ecclesiastical history – the break with Rome – and the shrines of Roman Catholic saints were dismantled, including that of Saint Wilfrid.

The Civil War of 1642 to 1649 further took its toll when Parliamentary soldiers broke in and smashed most of the beautiful medieval glass. Lack of maintenance again showed its ugly face and in 1660 the central tower fell through the roof. Again much damage was done, so much so that the twin spires of the west front were removed as a precautionary measure. A building of this size needs ongoing repair and restoration and it is a credit to the present generation that the Cathedral, after centuries of wear and tear and the traumas of two World Wars, is in such excellent condition today. The Minster is very dear to the heart of all true Riponians and long may it survive.

THE OXLEYS

I do remember that Hetty always used to steer us towards the impressive white memorial on the wall commemorating the Oxley family and depicting the heads of various members of the family in relief.

Sopwith Pup

The Oxleys

The Oxleys were a well-to-do and well connected family and are remembered by several memorials inside and outside the Cathedral, dating from at least the seventeenth century. In addition to being a family of surgeons, to select but a few of their family occupations, one was a master of Ripon Free Grammar School, one was an admiral, no less, in the Royal Navy, and one a pioneering pilot in World War One. One was son-in-law to Dean Robert Waddilove, hence closely connected with the Cathedral.

In 1916 Commander Christopher Oxley RN was part of a two-man crew, acting as observer, in a Sopwith fighter plane piloted by Flight Lieutenant Edward Dunning. On the Bulgarian coast two enemy machines were engaged at close range and were forced to retire. However, in the fracas, Dunning was injured but Oxley climbed out of his rear seat in mid-air, applied a tourniquet and flew the damaged plane back to base as the pilot stopped up holes in the fuel tank with his thumbs. The pilot whose life had been saved, as Squadron Leader Dunning, became the first man to land an aircraft, a Sopwith Pup, successfully on board a ship at sea; this was a perilous task because the large differences in speed of plane and ship caused tyres to burst on impact. Sadly, only one week after this successful feat in August 1917, Squadron Leader Dunning was drowned when he tried to repeat the manoeuvre. This time the aircraft wobbled off deck and plunged into the sea.

It so happened that one of Sopwith's chief designers was Herbert Smith, actually from my home village of Bradley. The designers worked hard to overcome the problems and tried to find alternatives for tyres which were prone to burst on landing, even experimenting with wooden skids in place of wheels.

I once had tea with Herbert Smith's widow at her home in Skipton. She died at the age of 106, but to the end fought long and hard to gain recognition for her husband's aviation skills.

SANCTUARY CROSS

To understand the significance of sanctuary crosses is to acknowledge that, generally speaking, punishment was much more severe in former days. One has only to reflect how, until comparatively recently, offenders could be transported to Australia for years for sheep stealing, in some cases, when they were merely trying to feed their starving families. In even earlier centuries rough justice was often meted out, and the threat of capital punishment was ever present.

Yes, there have always been, and always will be, people with criminal minds whatever their circumstances, but one has only to visualise the picture of a medieval offender pleading for sanctuary at a church door in a largely lawless England, to realise that the church offered some measure of respite to those otherwise without hope.

Only remaining sanctuary cross base at Sharow

SANCTUARY CROSS

The Sanctuary was a holy place where fugitives and criminals could take refuge without fear of arrest. In the thirteenth century there was a ring of eight sanctuary crosses marking out an area within a mile of the church in Ripon where fugitives could claim sanctuary. Only one sanctuary stone base remains in Ripon and this important relic can still be seen at Sharow.

Ripon was a chartered sanctuary town, which meant that for some thirty days and nights the fugitive was safely sheltered while his claim was being investigated, after which time various options were open to him.

LEPER CHAPEL

Poor lepers dwelt near, but shunned and alone,
Had to pick up their food from a hollowed-out stone.

61

Sometimes on our way along Magdalen Road, as we returned to Lickley Street, we would make a short detour to look at the leper chapel of Saint Mary Magdalen situated close to the roadside. Thanks to periodic restoration this ancient and historic building has survived, although the actual Leper House has long since been demolished. Hetty explained that she understood that, when lepers actually lived at the Leper House, the disease was so feared that the food for the inmates would be placed on or in a stone, a respectable distance away, to be collected later. Leprosy is said to have been introduced into this country after the Crusades, when English soldiers were sent out under the Banner of the Cross to recover Palestine from the Turks.

Leprosy

Leprosy was a terrible scourge in earlier times and sufferers were confined to leper houses and, if venturing outside, were compelled to wear bells warning of their approach. In some churches special windows or 'lepers' peeps' enabled them to follow the service without actually entering the church. The dreaded disease was often recognised when patches of white appeared on the skin. There was loss of feeling and parts of the limbs would fall away. After the fifteenth century the disease gradually disappeared, perhaps leaving the leper hospitals to deal with other infectious complaints. In spite of its reputation it is said that it was sometimes possible to live among lepers for many years before being contaminated. At Saint Mary Magdalen's Leper House, lepers and blind priests would also be given a ration of clothes each year and bread, beer, and flesh or fish daily. Almshouses have since been built nearby. There were three medieval hospital chapels in Ripon, Saint Mary Magdalen's, Saint John's and Saint Anne's, offering hospitality to the poor and sick and travellers in need. Sensibly, all were situated for convenience near river crossings.

THE WORKHOUSE

Hetty was a kindly soul. Occasionally we would accompany her on her weekly visit to the Workhouse, situated at the top of Allhallowgate. She carried a basket covered with a white cloth, and her mission was to visit an old woman of her acquaintance who was resident there. We children, however, were not allowed inside, and when Hetty disappeared through the entrance to the buildings beyond we had to make ourselves scarce until she reappeared.

Workhouse

The Workhouse was opened in 1854 to provide for 120 paupers in male and female blocks on the site of an earlier poorhouse. A vagrants' block was added later in 1876. The Workhouse was in use until 1929, round about the time I remember Hetty and her basket of baking. At that time it was still referred to as a 'workhouse' although the name had changed to 'poor law institution' in 1913. Workhouses were first set up for the old and destitute who received food and lodging in return for work done, although it is difficult to see how much work could be expected from the elderly. Sometimes the mentally ill and children too were accommodated. Conditions in workhouses generally were often fairly spartan and I have heard people of my parents' generation say that before the era of Old Age Pensions ordinary people felt obliged to save up all their working lives to avoid 'ending up in the workhouse', which was viewed as a disgrace to the family. The Ripon Workhouse eventually became an old people's home, but residents were removed to newer premises in 1974 and the vagrants' block later became the Poor Law Museum.

THE MARKET PLACE

M E. Lancaster

We had no problem considering what to do on Thursdays because Thursday was, and still is, market day in Ripon. On Thursday morning Gladys and I would accompany Hetty up Allhallowgate on our way to the Market Square. Between the Wars, Ripon Market seemed to us to be a busy place as we threaded our way through the various stalls. In my mind's eye I can still see where many of them were located, selling sweets, food, plants and flowers, bedding, haberdashery, jumpers and underwear, men's trousers, (few women wore trousers in those days), and those quirky little commodities which have a short life but which crop up from time to time, adding interest to the shopping experience. An outdoor market truly has an atmosphere all of its own.

Thursday has long been Market Day
Whenever the date falls,
We took our bags and wandered through
The many varied stalls.

Market Place

Fairs have been taking place in Ripon for centuries, as they have in many other ancient cities. Originally they were often connected with religious festivals and took place in the streets around old churches, where cattle were also bought and sold. Market records go back a long way and it is recorded that as early as the twelfth century a right to hold a fair in Ripon was granted by King Henry I. Eventually, when trading no longer took place in the streets fairs were held in the old Market Place. When more space was required, ground was cleared to build the present Market Square not far from the Old Market Place. Imposing as it is it does not equal in spaciousness many of the squares to be found in towns in northern France. Even so, bearing in mind present day traffic, early foresight has ensured that Ripon shoppers run less risk of being mown down than in many English towns where roadside markets are more exposed to passing traffic. The central Obelisk in the Square dates from 1702 when it was built by John Aislabie during his term of office as Mayor of Ripon.

Ancient hostelries add charm and a sense of history to towns and cities. Two hundred years ago, before the popularity of tea as a drink, there were over fifty inns and beer houses in Ripon. Most have disappeared, but thankfully two old coaching inns at least have survived. The old inn, the Black Bull, still fronts the Old Market Place and the Unicorn has survived, a dignified and historic presence in the present Market Square. The coaching era was roughly from the late eighteenth century to early mid-nineteenth century. Passengers were able to begin or end their journeys at old coaching inns and partake of refreshments and a bed for the night. Stabling facilities were provided and here horses could be changed. I am reminded at this point, that when about fourteen years old I had an overcoat with a large cape collar, fashionable at the time. My grandmother, who was born in 1851, remarked that it was 'just like a coachman's coat' which she obviously remembered. To think that I was a link with stage coaches – so beloved by designers of Christmas cards!

In good weather and reasonable road conditions, coaches would sometimes travel at the dizzy speed of 10 miles per hour, but the coming of the railways put paid to this form of transport. Links with the past still survive in Ripon. A bell ringer in the uniform of bygone days proclaims the market open at 11 a.m. by ringing the hand-bell which he carries. In today's climate of press-button controls and improved transport the market has been in full swing long before the official opening time.

THE WAKEMAN'S HOUSE

The Wakeman's house,
  in black and white
A leap from history's page,
Looking out upon the Square
  Recalls a former age.

For many years the Wakeman's House was a museum. I remember looking round with Cyril Lancaster who lived a few doors away from Jack and Hetty and who might have had some family connection with them. I do not remember any of the museum's exhibits but recall looking out onto the Square from an upstairs window.

Wakeman's House

A little further on from the Town Hall, at the corner of the Market Square stands the so-called Wakeman's House, as it was formerly believed that Hugh Ripley, the last Wakeman and the first Mayor of Ripon, lived here. This is not now believed to be the case, but the name has stuck and the property is still referred to as the Wakeman's House.

The old house, probably early sixteenth century in date, is an example of a timber-framed building. After years of neglect it was restored in the early 1920s, having narrowly escaped demolition. Since then it has served as café, warehouse, shop, tourist office and museum.

The Wakeman, or Watchman, had a year of office, during which time his duty was to preserve law and order. Helped by others, he kept a special night-watch with street patrols from horn-blowing at 9 o'clock until dawn. Compensation was paid to any victims of burglaries, but nothing is for free and householders were required to pay 2d per door as a sort of insurance and were required to keep their buildings adequately secured.

The Wakeman became first citizen of Ripon in his day and had other functions to perform. Hugh Ripley, the best known Wakeman of all, was also Mayor of Ripon three times. He died, aged 84, in 1637. At least his name has helped to preserve this once run-down, but now rather picturesque corner of old Ripon.

THE HOUSE OF CORRECTION AND PRISON

71

We were not the only child visitors to have early memories of holidays in Ripon. In adult life my family and I lived in the country on the Yorkshire—Lancashire border. We had some very good neighbours whose children were roughly the same age as ours, and there was much to-ing and fro-ing across the fields. In the course of conversation it transpired that the mother, Dorothy, had also, as a child, stayed with her relations in Ripon. This was most likely at about the same time as we were there, although we did not know her in those days. Whereas we stayed in Lickley Street, she was more upmarket and stayed not far away with her relations at the police station in St. Marygate, an historic building which had once been Ripon's House of Correction. She used to say that sometimes when the officer's wife cooked for the family she would cook for the prisoners in the police station as well, which meant that they were well fed. This was apparently greatly appreciated by the inmates. Hardly a punishment!

The House of Correction and Prison

The House of Correction, a pleasant-looking building with rows of mullioned windows, was opened in 1684 and operated until 1816 when the adjacent grim-looking prison was added. The original building became the governor's residence.

The House of Correction dealt mainly with young men and petty offenders and aimed to tackle the problem of vagrancy and reluctance to work by attempting to change attitudes. Meanwhile, for a long time conditions in the prison were less than salubrious and punishment on the treadmill was common. The tread-wheel was turned by prisoners constantly walking on steps on the surface of a revolving upright wheel.

FAIRY STEPS
OR
FAIREY STEPS

M.E.L.

73

One afternoon Mabel Dunning, from the top shop, and I went to the Fairy Steps which were to be found in the pleasant wooded area at the end of Borrage Lane.

The Steps

Apparently this long flight of steps up a steep bank had existed before World War One but when the area became part of the vast Ripon army camp the steps were rebuilt and improved. It is said that the concrete strips up either side facilitated the movement of gun carriages and maybe tanks, while the 'push-and-shove' brigade were able to gain a foothold on the steps up the middle. There is some controversy as to how the Fairy Steps were so named. It has been said that a certain individual surnamed Fairey was a designer of military equipment including a Fairey Tank and that the steps were named after him. Certainly Fairey designed military equipment, but this was mainly in the Second World War and I have found no evidence of a Fairey Tank, so maybe we will have to settle for the name of the two-winged variety.

Wartime

Ripon played an important part as a garrison town in the two World Wars. A vast army camp covering one thousand acres was created in 1915, when large numbers of tents and huts lined the roadsides. Miles of roads and footpaths had to be built, water supplies secured, and sewage and drainage attended to. Furthermore, accommodation for a sizeable workforce had to be found. The increased population no doubt brought welcome trade into the town, but this also meant that there was an increase in drunkenness and disorderliness. Ripon, to me, seemed a strange choice for a garrison town, as the Cathedral was an obvious landmark, but overall the plan worked very well and the Cathedral came to no harm.

WILFRED OWEN

Futility

Move him into the sun —
Gently its touch awoke him once,
At home, whispering of fields unsown.
Always it woke him, even in France,
Until this morning and this snow.
If anything might rouse him now
The kind old sun will know.

Think how it wakes the seeds, —
Woke, once, the clays of a cold star.
Are limbs, so dear-achieved, are sides,
Full-nerved — still warm — too hard to stir?
Was it for this the clay grew tall?
— O what made fatuous sunbeams toil
To break earth's sleep at all?

Wilfred Owen

The First World War was a time of unbelievable carnage, when scarcely a family escaped unscathed. Even today, and after yet another World War, the scale of the slaughter still evokes an acute sense of shock. One has only to visit the war cemeteries of the Somme, with their serried ranks of thousands and thousands of headstones and crosses, to realise the pain and suffering experienced by the dead and wounded and the sense of loss and devastation for every family represented there, of whatever nationality.

Wilfred Owen

The horrors of war gave rise to a spate of First World War poets, of whom Wilfred Owen was one. Born in Oswestry, he was the eldest of four children. In adult life he became a teacher of English at Bordeaux in 1913 and a year later became a private teacher to a prosperous family in the Pyrenees. He enlisted in late 1915 and was trained in England. As an officer based in Ripon, he lived on Borrage Lane for only about 3 months from March to June 1918. His war experience was rather short with only five weeks on the line, but all his war poetry was based on this experience and he became a friend of that other Great War poet, Siegfried Sassoon.

Owen, though patriotic, wrote graphic poetry describing the horror of war in all its brutal reality. His poetry does not make comfortable reading, but that was scarcely the intention. Perhaps his most well known poem is 'Dulce et decorum est pro patria mori', in which he deplored the assumption that it is sweet and right to die for one's country. One of his poems, 'Futility', was reputedly written in Ripon. It is doubtful if Wilfred Owen even knew that he would become an acclaimed war poet for he was killed, aged 25, in the final stages of the War, and only one week before the signing of the Armistice. What a waste of life, and in his case a waste of talent.

SPA GARDENS

Now and again on sunny days –
If loth to travel far,
We found a seat, or sauntered through
The gardens of the Spa.

Occasionally, on a warm summer's day we would wander through the delightful Spa Gardens and find a seat to watch the world go by.

Spa Gardens

Ripon's stylish Spa buildings convey an air of opulence and laid-back gentility. However, the Spa dream in Ripon did not develop in quite the way anticipated.

To begin with, Ripon did not have the same natural amenities as nearby Harrogate. There was a source of curative mineral water in Stonebridgegate but that was considered inadequate for development purposes; instead, the Marquis of Ripon proposed bringing piped mineral water from his estate at Studley.

In 1900 a field was acquired to be developed into a pump room spa followed with gardens and bandstand. In 1905 the Spa opened and the Spa Hotel opened in 1909. All seemed set for a promising future, but the whole idea never really took off and in 1947 plans for Ripon as a Spa Treatment Centre were abandoned.

However, fashions and demands change. Before that there had been a growing demand for a swimming bath, and in 1936 part of the building was converted to more useable swimming baths.

STREET NAMES

I love some of the old street names in Ripon even though some have changed from their original meaning. Blossomgate still conjures up a pleasant quiet road untroubled by traffic, as does Duck Hill which hasn't seen a duck for a day or two! Barefoot Street, though apparently changed in name from Berfordgate (originally Barley Ford), still reminds one of the days when children really did go barefoot because the price of a pair of shoes was beyond the means of many. Indeed, as recently as 1906 the Mayor of Ripon drew attention to the increasing number of children being sent to school without shoes.

Quite a few old cities have a Finkle Street, which I imagined must refer to an old mint, as 'Finkle' has a kind of tinkling sound, but apparently it denotes a winding road, curve or corner of which there would be many in the old days.

Ripon Street Names

Old City names still tell a tale,
Of interest to relate,
When, linked to Ripon's ancient past
An 'entrance' was a 'gate'.

Was Bondgate where no freeman lived?
Their lives controlled by others,
Sad lives of toil and servitude
For fathers, sons and brothers.

Along Priest Lane the clerics walked –
Allhallowgate sounds holy,
And signifies an age of faith,
The Sabbath – God's day solely.

On Barefoot Street did urchin play?
With sister or with brother
Maybe content in scraps and rags
Because he knew no other.

Sometimes a name is all that's left
To turn time's hidden key,
On Duck Hill stood a mill and pond
Where duckling wandered free.

And Blossomgate so brings to mind
A pastoral tree-lined city scene
With narrow roads and high stone walls
And cottages between.

These names belong to former days
When Ripon's die was cast.
They signify an age long gone
And link us to the past.

MEL

OUT AND ABOUT

On a summer's evening what better than to take a long walk in the evening sunshine along the river banks? Turning off Magdalen Road, we followed a footpath along the bank of the Ure, continuing to the confluence of Ure and Skell when we turned right towards the city, and back via Fishergreen and the cricket field, now relocated. Somehow the wide Ure always seemed more menacing than the friendly Skell and we dare not stray too near the wider stretches of the Ure in case we vanished into the unknown depths.

All this talk of rivers brings me to another memory. Turning left before the North Bridge and alongside the river bank brought us to the boathouse with wooden benches outside where cups of tea were dispensed. Here, rowing boats could be hired, a popular pastime for a summer's evening and a favourite venue for couples on their first date. There is no longer boating on the Ure which somehow seemed to be a 'must' in those days adding to the atmosphere of a picturesque cathedral city.

Ripon Races, however, have survived. If anything was happening, Jack and Hetty saw that we did not miss out, and I remember being taken to the Races – but all that remains in my memory of this event is a stallholder dishing out hot peas! Why, I wonder are our memories so selective?

I remember the races at Ripon,

The event I remember with ease,

Not the horses, nor running, nor wagers,

But a stallholder selling hot peas.

Ripon Races

Ripon Races have a long history and were first established in 1714 on High Common. The venue was changed several times until finally in 1899 a new Ripon Race Company was founded on the eastern edge of the city, near the River Ure. The first meeting was held in 1900 and this site is still in use today.

MOVING ON

When we are children — at least those of us who were lucky enough to be brought up in a stable environment — we think that we shall always be cocooned by the same cosy relationships. How wrong we can be! Looking back now, I find that there are very few still around who helped to shape my life.

My gentle and considerate brother, Leonard (named after an Uncle Leonard who was killed on the Somme), had a normal healthy and happy childhood, but he developed an unforeseen illness and died one week before his eighteenth birthday and from which I felt my parents never fully recovered. My cousin, Gladys, my Ripon companion, passed away later in life, along with older relations, which, after all, is only to be expected. The story is repeated in Ripon as elsewhere. When Jack died after retirement Hetty moved to live in Russell Dixon Square. Here, she was very comfortable in her old age with everything to hand that she could wish for, but she left her heart in Lickley Street. Even the children we played with in those far off days have run their race.

Just as people change and move on, so places change, sometimes for the better, sometimes for worse. What changes have I noticed in and around Ripon after so many decades? Happily, although there has been a great deal of new modern housing built since the War, the heart of the city does not at first glance appear to have changed all that much. The Obelisk still towers over the Market Square and the builders of the supermarket onto the Square have to be applauded for the discrete way in which the entrance has been positioned.

The Wakeman's House still stands in a prime position reminding us of a former age, having survived demolition by the skin of its teeth, although the adjoining shop has gone.

As a child I was very partial to ice cream and well remember Mastermans selling ice cream from the Square as well as from their shop in Allhallowgate which was in business for many years. The chip shop I mentioned earlier has vanished without trace from the junction with Priest's Lane. The name 'Allhallowgate' suggests a medieval road steeped in history and it is something of a shock to see the new post-war be-railinged flats which have sprung up near the top of this ancient thoroughfare; though handy for the town and Square, these hardly inspire a sense of history.

Ripon has made its mark on the educational scene. The ancient Grammar School, refounded in 1555, still soldiers on and has survived so far in spite of the reshaping of education. The women's teacher-training college, however, has ceased to exist and the substantial buildings have become a housing development. The College must have done sterling service in its day as I personally have known a few women teachers very grateful for the training which they received in Ripon. The railway had a short life; built in 1848 it only lasted a few decades and services ended in 1967.

Ripon has done sterling service throughout two World Wars, and many soldiers of the First World War remembered Ripon for being the place where they were finally demobbed. There is still an army presence of Royal Engineers in Ripon, but nowhere on the scale of wartime days, when tents sprung up in their thousands and the city echoed to the tramp of marching feet.

Fishergreen was set in a delightful rural riverside scene with two sets of stepping stones, one set of which is now disappearing beneath the waters. However, I have to say that since new houses have sprung up on the site Fishergreen has lost some of its magic for me.

To satisfy the need for evening relaxation there was also the cinema, a little way down Kirkgate and not far from the Market Square. There was no television in those days but as in every town popular cinemas have had to bow to the TV and the cinema is now a nightclub.

In the past, before mechanisation, Ripon was renowned for making spurs, saddle trees, cloth and lace, but as times change so do occupations. Along with the names of Riponians who have diversified and expressed their talents otherwise or elsewhere, we can add that of Bruce Oldfield, a Barnardo's boy who attended Ripon Grammar School and who has become a notable fashion designer.

There are numerous societies that enrich life in Ripon. A thriving Civic Society and Historical Society keep the history of the city in mind. Other activities are catered for by the Golf Club, the Spa Baths and the Marina, cricket, football and rugby clubs, and the Leisure Centre. For those musically inclined there is a choir and Ripon City Band. No doubt there are other activities equally as important. After a lapse, Morris Dancing has been rekindled; it is now a popular pastime and healthy activity. The Ripon dancers in their colourful costumes and bowler hats decorated with fresh flowers strike a cheerful note as they dance outside in various northern towns and cities, and they have even been known to travel as far afield as Prague to display their skills.

The moorland road to Ripon has had to adapt to changes in line with everything else, but thankfully large tracts of uncultivated heather-clad moorland still remain. Here and there radio masts and wind turbines intrude upon the sky-line, along with the now familiar 'golf-balls', a modern version of the brochs and beacons of long ago.

Gladys was a few years older than I was, and our yearly visits to Ripon came to an abrupt end when a young man appeared on the scene (whom she subsequently married). We were left, however, with a legacy of happy memories.

Today there is often hardly any difference between one town centre and another. The same multiple stores with similar functional architecture grace many of our town centres, but Ripon at least retains much of its individuality. As a child I remember reading the inscription boldly inscribed in huge letters in the cornice in front of the Town Hall in 1886 : 'EXCEPT YE LORD KEEP YE CITTIE YE WAKEMAN WAKETH IN VAIN'. This is adapted from Psalm 127 in King James' version of the Bible from the second part of verse 1, which reads, 'Except the Lord Keep the city, the watchman waketh but in vain'. To read it gave me much pleasure in those early days and it gives me pleasure today. Somehow it seems to remind us that, even in these modern days of technology, travel, computerisation and materialism, Ripon's history is steeped in the legacy of Saint Wilfrid and there could still be a hidden spiritual thread running through life if we seek to acknowledge it.

The days of our youth have gone scurrying past.

The voices we heard are no more,

But our childhood lives on

If we venture to peep

Through memory's half open door.

Bibliography :

The Memorials of Ripon Cathedral	Ripon Cathedral Office
An Illustrated History of Ripon	Maurice Taylor – Stratus Books
Northumbrian Saints	E. C. S. Gibson
Early British Kingdoms	David Nash Ford
'St. Wilfrid' – The Catholic Encyclopaedia	Arthur Barnes
Echoes from Ripon's Past	Editor: Mike Younge – Ripon Local Studies Research Centre
The Historical Streets of Ripon	Maurice Taylor – Ripon Civic Society
A Ripon Record 1887 – 1986	Ripon Civic Society – Phillimore
Herbert Smith – Aircraft Designer par Excellence (manuscript)	Robin Platt
Poems by Thomas Hood	
Poems by Wilfred Owen	

Books by the same author :

The Tempests of Broughton

Across Throup's Bridge (with M. Throup)

Bradley Long Since

Looking Back at Skipton

West Craven Patchwork (with D. Carthy)

A Way of Life Gone By (with D. Carthy)

The Changing Years

They Were There!

History of Bracewell Parish and Church

From Foe to Friend